GLEANING THE S

by

Nan Dalton

Typeset and Published
by
The National Poetry Foundation
(Reg Charity No 283032)
27 Mill Road
Fareham
Hants PO16 0TH
(Tel/Fax: 01329 822218)

D1437957

Consort Print Services
Consort Court, High Street
Fareham, Hants PO16 7AL
(Tel 01329 822530)

Sponsored by Rosemary Arthur

Cover drawing by Michael Taylor

Edited by Johnathon Clifford

Poetry previously published in *Pause, Teign Verse* (Devon County Libraries) and *Otter*, and has been broadcast on BBC Radio Devon and Dorset. *Snake, Toad and the Long Crippled Grass Snake* was joint third in the Library of Avalon Competition 1994 and *Bournvita for Two* accepted by The Imperial War Museum for its poetry collection.

ISBN 1 870556 89 5

CONTENTS

* * *

To Ann and Theo

CHILDPROOF

Our third
and suddenly
I become childproof,
resistant to tiny fingers,
dimpled smiles.

Other people's children
can't win me,
can't reach me.
"Ugly little thing"
I think, steeling myself
to stay polite.

But now I see
a composite of faces,
faces known and loved,
thought gone forever
but brought alive
once more
in his brown gaze.

He grips
my outstretched finger,
crows his way into my heart
and, defences down,
I become vulnerable to,
not proof against,
his childish charms.

EXCESS BAGGAGE

Years on and my response
is automatic
and I brace myself
for yet another
encounter of the human kind,
hope this one won't be
full of stress, promise
myself to stay remote,
ration time, ignore needs,
stay landlady hard.

Check facilities,
finish just in time.
She smiles but not her eyes,
puts out a cooling hand
and before I know it
we're sitting side by side
"You don't want to hear . . ."
then tells me anyway -
a suicide, a death,
the urge to get away.

Ashamed I murmur
platitudes, explain
the best place to eat
show her on the map
"Go now, don't leave it
late! Our town's kind enough
to strangers but be sure
to be back here by eight!"
I bite back experiences
shared with other guests.

Next day we say goodbye.
I press a talisman,
my card, into her hand.
Her words, her story,
stay in my head. Rapidly
I strip the bed. Refill
the coffee jar. Wonder
is it meant that they
should come and leave their
excess baggage here?

INCHCOULTER
(For Elizabeth Renier)

February and blossoms burgeon
on these knurled and twisted limbs,
scent hangs in clouds
where once Inchcoulter stood.

Its Cottage coach house home
where carriage horse names
'Lady, Captain, Ginger' still
graced the stable loft.
And there, beyond
this cherry tree,
one August day we met,
drank gin, ate sandwiches.

Felt words waft skyward
through summer heat
on an unexpected breeze,
and conversation
bounced along a row of beans,
tomatoes staked against
a southern wall, as we
sat close to a statued pool.

Then, she began to read,
pass on her skills,
made people come alive,
involved us in a loving tryst -
pounding horses raced a storm
to deliver mail - and she showed
us how to use nuances, phrases,
set to work for children
to read in bed,

Now it was our turn to read
out fumbling words
against a background
of flowering treasure
and this tree (leafy then
in summer measure)
as we struggled to climb
the literary ladder.

February again and we stand
upon this empty plot
still signed 'Inchcoulter'
remember all we gained
when she lived near.

5

BLAME THE SUPERMARKETS

. . . for merging all four seasons
and turning them into one
giving me strawberries at Christmas
and everything under the sun
is available from Egypt and Chile,
California, Holland and Spain.
So I'm wearing shorts in February,
sweaters from Iceland in July;
cooking lobster in October
while I've waved local yoghurt goodbye.

Swapped Cheddar cheese for Ricotta,
dress my salad in *Fromage Frais*
while Frenchmen in Calais
eat clotted cream from Devon all day
and, when squid and french fries come along,
I wash them down with glasses of Bulgarian Sauvignon.

Please supermarket bosses listen,
restore my reason and
give me back my sense of season

. . . keep Spring for cabbage, salsify,
chocolate eggs and hot cross buns.
Confine strawberries to June and Wimbledon.
Harvest onions and apples in September,
and don't above all, don't, bring out
mincepies and crackers until December.

MEMOING (MIMING)

Half term and they drive up the ramp,
stop by protective railings,
apply their brakes and rest.
Angle heads towards Tom
as he activates the looms,

tells his grandmother's story
in thick dialect of the women
grouped and smiling on the end wall
of this factory room.

"A bell set off clatter of clogs
as they raced across stone floor
to the clack of racks of reels in rows.
Reminds you of industrial terraces?"

"Their fingers flew - inches away
from broken limbs - to feed the grabbing
greedy cotton machines." He pauses
"Memoing out their lives with eyes
and lips all for a pound a week,
less a shilling for gaslight and steam."

Tom switches off belts driving
temperamental steam machines named
Ethel, Madge, Irene,
and it's silence now
that hurts our ears.

Hands, eager to be off, swing wheels
away from protective railings
but, at my request, pause to brake again;
smile as I flash my camera
then race each other up the ramp.

THE FINAL SHIFT

Blindfold the horses came.
Some ran, some stood their ground.
"I'll never forget the heat
from the horses' breath
as I fell beneath their feet."

Jason looked up
"What happened, what happened then?"

"I came to, son, came to
to the rattle of nightsticks,
the sound of bricks
on riot shields."

A miner looks out of the frame
pockets supporting heavy hands
charcoal and wash reflecting
the end of the final shift.

Jason studies the picture
where it hangs in the half empty
room. "Why did you strike, Dad?
We've to do a project at school."

Tom brushes a weary hand
across his frozen face,
"I've told you, son,
told you again and again."

Irene attacks a pile of sheets
"strike pay for a family like ours
were thirteen pound a week,
so we stole key to Parish Room
and there baked gifts of meat."

She pushes away a strand of hair,
hair a premature gray.
"Tell him, Tom, tell him
how armoured cars broached
colliery gate."

Tom took up the tale
"We'd have starved rather than cross
picket line, and it was rumour,
rumour that khaki was turning to blue,
that sparked miners' rage."

His eyes flashed as Jason
played on his computer game.
"We stood, stone solid,
stone solid before closed pit gate."

His eyes filled now, body tense.
Irene hurried across the room.
Jason, bored now, edged towards the door.
"I'll be off, then" he said,
but neither of them heard.

THE GALLOPERS

Gray towers soft against
an Exeter sky, conceal a tree,
an Epiphany tree,
clothing the Cathedral
in white candled light,

And in Solstice short hours
I search for the spark
to start this event
cross History's green
drawn to the Guidhall
by piped organ sound

Where the Gallopers prance
around and around,
nostrils flaring,
eyes brilliant and bold.
Children, hair streaming, cling
to harness of blue, red and gold

Their chargers flying in pairs,
rearing and bucking
to old seaside airs.
Brass poles twist in a bright
burst of sun and flags fly
from a striped awning above.

Mirrors, beaded and bevelled,
flash and reflect
marionettes playing trumpet and drum,
while grandmothers clutch children
who came to see Santa
but ride the Gallopers instead
and shout out in glee

"Christmas, Christmas,
Christmas has come."

FLOOD

Sara heard a sandbag hit her step,
remembered,
called in Ginger out preening in the yard,
made tea in flasks, sliced bread.
Moved photos of Stan in battledress,
Kevin and Kim in trim schoolwear,
dragged a mattress down the narrow stair.

It was a cloudburst late that afternoon
tipped the balance, caused the Lemon
to swell, drown peat bog and heather,
roar down the Sigford valley,
submerge ancient bridge and ford,
hang grazing sheep in willow forks,
set mill wheels creaking.

At sea a spring tide built beyond the bar
surged in past Teignmouth's Ness to
smash pleasure boats against the Quay,
race under Shaldon Bridge, slap river banks,
destroy kingfisher nests, lift herons
to rise high above the railway
and shetler in the trees.

Sara waited till she heard the slap
of water as it swept along her street,
watched salty sludge slide
under her front door ro cover flowered
carpets, reach old marks in the hall.
Then, grabbed Ginger and retreated
up the narrow stair.

The two rivers met in Bank Street,
swept shoes from drowned shop doorways,
poured past The Globe to breach
Queen Street and Courtenay.
Douse fires in baker's ovens,
set free a grand piano to dance
back across the market square.

Ginger cleaned mud from his coat.
Sara pressed firemen to sandwiches and tea
while the moon rose over Newton, where
an eerie silence filled the air,
showing Bushell Ward and Bradley
once again divided as they'd been
in 1673.

VICTIM SUPPORT

They say
"You're mad to keep
an open house,
share with strangers,
pretend today's
the same sane scene."

And afterwards

They said
"You only have yourself
to blame."
But then they didn't share
the pain of precious pieces
gone to buy a fix.

And when I walk
beyond the tracks
to glean the seasons as they pass
they say,
"You're asking for it."

And afterwards,

Would they shrug and say
"She only had herself to blame."
Refuse to help,
retreat behind locked doors
into the bleakness
of their hearts.

FINAL ACCOUNT

Coming to terms,
absenting strong warm hands,
sorting, sifting,
drawing up stray strands.

Checking customer
wedding orders,
cards enclosed by
deep black borders.

Searching upstairs
among his things,
ash dusted desk top,
autographed coffee rings.

Smoothing out creases
in folded down pages
where a magus conjured
credits, debits, wages.

Ringing up memories
on an ancient cash machine
as out of date
as his last campaign.

Cold smoke brings tears,
flames lick a long held brief,
consign the past to
a balance sheet of grief.

BOURNVITA FOR TWO
(Forces Sweetheart Exhibition, Imperial War Museum 1993)

. . . in a honeymoon bed, not champagne
on a hotel bill, a khaki tunic on the floor
entwined with a shiver of caminicks
made by a WRAF from net curtains
the night before . . .

This ad in a Sunday magazine
draws me onto a London coach when paper
boys are still delivering. I brave
a bomb hoax, walk Westminster Bridge
pass 'Big Bertha' and on
into the War Museum.

A lump forms quickly in my throat
as I read battered letters in copper
plate from gas filled trenches.
A lump that grows as I view a soldier's
pouch of leather holding a baby shoe,
a smiling portrait of a shingle
haired young woman.

Anger replaces tears as Sam swanks
of conquests in a Flanders village.
Emily sends love, spelt out in black
suddenly switching to red, the day
his philandering comes to an end
in a shell hole full of mud
and rats.

I move on pass gas masks, campaign ribbons,
gold epaulettes, white feathers,
to a letter marked 'missing in action'.
Attached is a black bordered missive
from his commanding officer
promising a posthumous
V.C. instead.

Abandoning horrors from Hilter's war,
and 'the war to end all wars'
of twenty years before,
I go down a slope into a trench.
The feel of it I'll always
remember.

> Gas smoke urine blood excreta
> fraught with fear as poised
> on a firing step men wait
> for the officer's whistle.

I shut off my senses,
blot out the smell of cordite,
the crump of shells,
think of the Uncle I never met
the one who, to me, will
always be twenty.

FABERGÉ

Slowly we circle glass octagons
in a dimly lighted hall and I think
of Russian Winters when nights lasted till
ten next morning from three the day before
and Trotsky talked revolution, then fled abroad.

Russian music, sombre as Tolstoy's
'War and Peace' swallows us at the entrance
door. Blown up photos of Tsars, Kings,
and delicate plant designs
for jewellery fill the walls.

Elgar's 'Crown Imperial' establishes
the British link reinforced by enamelled
photoframes of Tsar Nicholas and George the Fifth;
cousins dressed in sailor suits, bearded, they stand
like twins by dairy sheds at Sandringham.

I admire a silver samovar, but have to wait
for the fabled egg. See cutlery taken to
a 'different' Siberia on Royal Summer trips
while grain crops failed and Russian workers
marched, and shouted "Give us bread."

War came and Fabérge's factory stopped
making gew gaws for the Tsar.
changed to hand grenades instead.
The German sounding St. Petersburg became Petrograd;
still Krapenskaya danced and Chaliapin sang.

Women workers faced the Cossack terror in July,
then Winter snows and revolution came on fast
and Russian troops, brainwashed by Isvestia,
changed sides, deserted Allied battle-lines
as Bolshevik 'truth' quickly turned to lies.

At last I gain the glass, see Nicholas's gift
to Alexandrovna in true Fabérge tradition -
an egg of gold with a surprise concealed inside.

As a child my father told me how to win the war.
Germany sent in a train with Lenin sealed inside.

Soon Tsar Nicholas became 'Comrade Tsar',
and found wanting by his people, was shot
in a lonely basement, his family by his side.
His son, a haemophiliac took longer to die,
Anastasia, it's said, was clubbed to death.

Sobered by the past, dazzled by porphyry,
enamel, jade; I drink coffee in the exhibition bar.
Recall the night the Berlin Wall was smashed
and democracy for Russians
arrived at last.

THE DESK

. . . sits against the studio wall,
gold timber dark with age,
awaiting knotted hands
to come to rest, heavy
on the writing slope.

Phrases, themes, cadenzas,
lie pigeonholed against the muse,
burning to be used, seeking arousal.
Fingers seize a pen,
shake out larksong
in splashes of black ink.

Notate striated wings
to brush against the studio glass,
fly a canvas of summer light,
reach the upper atmosphere
to trill on strings and hover there,
a speck of black.

Drawers warped with the weight
of manuscript, pour out seasongs,
folk tunes in three four,
a city symphony,
a serenade for orchestra and voice.

Hands sift and sort grained harmonies,
drum out rhythmn with fingertips,
stop to orchestrate the bird
earthward on cloudcapped wings
to nest among moorland heath.

And we, our spirits high,
watch the same fingers
close the desk
move across the studio
to try this fantasia
on waiting contrapuntal keys.

THE READING

Welcomed to a hotel room -
twin-sets chintz and coffee cups
white co-respondent shoes
yacht club blazers chinking bracelets -
I look beyond into the bay.

'We', I wave at Mary, Claire, met
through writing circles
studied Shakespeare, Manley Hopkins,
Larkin, Keats (I pause, wishing
I'd not begun this way).

I clear a drying throat, begin
a piece approved of by Greenpeace,
next comes *Rush Hour*, bang up to date,
then descriptive lines on Venice,
Sunday trips to car boot sales.

We three combine on country weekends,
wine, a sunless holiday in Tuscany,
end with *Reunion* which gets a laugh
followed by polite applause
and then, they come towards us.

I hold my breath, what reaction
to expect? Demands for books lying
in a pristine pile perhaps?
Requests for autographs?
Surreptitiously I reach for a pen.

"The street you mention in that piece
about a family." "Yes?"
"I know the woman who lives at No 63."
She beams then fades while others
finger books. Our hostess
says

"I'll buy your book, but not today."
Hesitates, then blurts out "What I really want
is you to read *my* work, it's prose
but all my own. Or,
just tell me where to send it!"

ARRIVALS

I waited all through April
when dull days depressed my spirit
river mist masked Haldon's hills
and traffic torched its way
across the town.

She, Gemini and rebel,
cheeky, talented, a loving fidget,
had set herself new goals,
made me a special
promise.

And so I waited while cherry
blossom lit up gravestones
on Wolborough Hill
and listened for Spring's
herald.

Could green-radio yet be wrong,
crops stay uncut from under
nesting birds and set-aside
see nature's balance
once more restored?

Still no message came until
the end of May. Just when
I'd given up all hope of Spring,
house martins soared above
on swept back wings

checked housing and conversed
in high pitched screams.
Encouraged, again I walked the hill
and there it came cool, clear,
unmistakeable, across fresh flowered
fields. Confident, brash and
full of cheek - *cuckoo*

an omen perhaps?

I didn't linger, but ran
to claim the message
on my answerphone;
"A Gemini called Theo
with her delicate tapering
painter's fingers."

CRYSTAL PALACE 1851-1936
(Inspired by Victoria's Albert and built to house the Great
[Industrial] Exhibition in Hyde Park, then removed to
Upper Norwood. Described as "the fresh air suburb out of
the reach of valley fogs")

Sundays, then, we climbed a hill
at   Havering-atte-Bower
to see the sun reflecting
primary colours from
flashing crystal towers.
Older now I tread the site
of parallel polygons,
find only Egyptian sphinxes
guarding mile long
empty terraces.

See people of mixed race
stroll where men from Rotherhithe
and Bow took part in cricket,
archery; wooed Sunday sweethearts
on a boating lake, and children
rode Professor Owen's
Plesiosaurus, Iguanodon,
nightly in their dreams.

Ada longed for a "mehogany" whatnot,
a box of Sheffield plate.
Bands and fountains played
until a workman's cigarette
caused a conflagration more spectacular
than any staged event, reduced
my childish fantasy of wrought iron
and crystal glass into fused lead.

Now I stare across London's arc;
relive days in typing pools,
nights promenading concerts,
search the horizon for that
high Sunday viewing place.

THE END OF THE AFFAIR

It is not you I miss
although you held my days,
it is the shape of hours spent, that's changed;
the time I have where once there was none left.
I fought for space and won, but now must pay.

Our time together holds me in a backward glance,
the pain of loss too great for tears
turns back the clock to other partings,
all bound up in acts of love.

We stay polite, pass gifts from holidays,
no longer share Swiss chocolate, French wine,
or a lover's kiss.

NO DOOM OR GLOOM

. . . she'd said in that positive way she had,
a way of instilling hope in all who shared
her thoughts, a voice that wrapped one round
with warmth.

"That party will be for you. I want there
to be lots of touching, hugging, enjoying
food and wine, good conversation,
getting in the party mood."

We did as we'd been told - shared memories
with families, put faces to friends
and colleagues who, until today,
had just been names.

Tried her knack of turning a sandwich
in a bar into a five star lunch, a rain ruined
holiday into fun, as sparky as Judy striking
Punch. A Sunday conversation on the telephone
would leave one feeling higher than the moon . . .

And so we drank and ate the buffet food
without a sense of grief, just huge relief
that all her pain was gone. Tears put on hold
we hung onto her brief, not admitting to each other
that life could never ever be the same.

YELLOW
(*Impressions of a visit to Berry Pomeroy Castle*)

Yellow reflects the April sun
mirrored in drifts of bright kingcups,
watered by the Gatcombe mere
and a lizard basks on a fallen oak
close to a Castle's mute mill pond.

Ruins stand, stark silhouettes,
pillaged by villagers long ago,
built by Henri de Pomerai and used
as a setting for Edward Seymour's
refuge from intrigues at Court.

I study roofless walls pitted
with joist holes, blackened grates,
read information boards which tell
me how Sir John Soane built a copy
of Seymour's house in 1812 Italianate.

Bells ring in my brain, of course,
John Soane's house is now a museum
in Lincoln's Inn. I forget statuary,
artefacts, his drawings, bound vellum,
remember only drapes of yellow.

Yellow silk that sent me roaring home
to paint the same warm colour
on the walls of my own small sitting room.
Christine and I discuss this deja vu,
how Edward Seymour, Duke of Somerset,

Lord Protector, employed four hundred men,
built in London, Wiltshire, Bedford,
and here in Devon. Imagine the sun
that shines on us today shone on
Edward's execution on Tower block.

We pause, descend deep dungeons
where a sister languished in the cause
of jealous love, then search in vain
for Margaret's ghost. I climb a walkway
to the roof, look down on ramparts

where mailed and mounted brothers
jumped together to their deaths;
a cold wind brings the taste of blood,
a stench of night visitors
fills the air.

MESSAGE TO MY MOTHER

. . . and still I long and long to know the words
you wrote me fifty years ago. Wrote and sent
that Christmas tucked inside a handmade bra.
If only they'd been kept, not thrown away unread.

My careless act has haunted me throughout my life;
now forces me back to childhood days. I seek out
the album with its faded sepia print. The family
group dressed in our best with fishing rods
crossed over childish nets. You wearing
a proud smile beneath a dark cloche hat.

That day we trawled the lake, oblivious of what
was to come, the lost battle for your mind
against a background of cavalry mown down by tanks.
Dad's tears and workplace blown away by bombs
while, labelled, gas masked, I rode a train.

I turn the pages, there in black and white
stands Lizzie Chapman, my suitcase in her hands.
"Come along my dear," she says, and leads me to a cottage
over threatened sun-baked fields, wraps me in her family
who fill my empty room with photographs, her son on leave
from training sorties over France, her daughter, my friend.

No-one came for me that Christmas as, dress pulled tight
by growing breasts, I undid your package to find
a handmade bra, and tucked inside a sheet of verse.
Now, hot with shame, I remember how I hid your words
from Lizzie Chapman's kind enquiring gaze.
"It's nothing - just wrapping." I think that's what I said.

I close the album return to my self elected task.
Is this your hand now guiding mine?
Your mind which sends fresh images?

SNAKE, TOAD, AND THE LONG CRIPPLED GRASS SNAKE
(*Leechwells,   Totnes*)

Chain mailed figures, white surcoats
crossed in red, kneel beside the rail to celebrate
a victory over desert infidel,
unknowing the legacy brought back by sea -
respecter of neither man nor woman, high born or low
- a bacillus eating limb or face.

Bell sounds warn the town beware the one
who hobbles, crawls on stunted limbs,
caped and gowned in black hood drawn tight
about a hairless sunken, ulcered face;
the husky voice escapes through wasted lips
"Alms, alms for pity's sake."

At Leechwells the figure stops, looks about,
implores the Gray Lady of the Wells to cure
his ills, chooses between the three stone sinks
then stoops to bathe his tortured limbs
in Snake, Toad, Long Crippled Grass Snake,
then retraces his steps to Maudlin's Halls.

Come holy days, eight lazars leave the hospital,
process along the Leper's Walk,
take turns to peer through Mary's Chancel squint
to see a Crusader receive the wafer, host, from
a Holy Priest, while all the time they clutch
a leopard lily[1] to their throats.

[1]*Leopard Lily (fritillaria meleagris) or lazar's bell from its likeness to the small
bell a lazar was forced to wear to warn of his approach.*

VALENTINE'S NIGHT

. . . and the snow came thick and fast,
muffled traffic sound, painted terraces
with a mask of white,
laid down a carpet on the hill.

Next day a secret population was betrayed
by padding paws, running, hopping claws,
brushmarks made by tails
marking garden path and wall.

I put on boots, crushed sparkling crystals
underfoot, broke icicles from catkined
hedgebanks by the path to church,
gasped at the picture hanging Breughel-like
above the town.

Squat figures glissading down;
red cheeked, raw fingered, they laughed.
Dogs barked and ran about. Tall figures came,
dragged sledges up the field, reclaimed their youth;
hurtled down beneath a sky of icy blue.
A small boy rolls in ecstacy, head-over-heals,
head-over-heels, then stuffs his mouth with snow.

I tear myself away, slip through the churchyard gate
where daffs sag beneath soft weight, then brush free
a rose red heart tagged with messages of love,
and a silent robin guards a sweetheart interred beneath.

IMAGES OF SPAIN

At ten we leave Granada for Seville -
city tenements for a sunflowered plain.
A black haired woman takes the space beside me
till we reach her stopping place. She treads
an unmarked track to a hacienda where eucalyptus
gives shade, and men shake ripe fruit from olive trees.
The plain fills up with grazing herds;
black bulls for men to fight in Picasso's ring.

Next day we leave behind packed city streets,
walk past brown velvet goats near Monachil.
"Ola" a young boy calls, as we climb hills,
find space to sleep. a place to eat ripe apricots.
We're invited into a village bar to drink cold beer,
while outside a tethered donkey staggers in the heat.

WINTER ON THE PROM

Sun splits cloud. Paints the horizon
with a silver edge. Gulls hang motionless.
Mufflered, Tom leads Dexter across the beach
where in Summer he'd be banned.
Both race towards a sandstone wedge,
watch yachts fight a five knot tide,
see clay boats hover at the bar and
locals fish for salmon on the slack.
Gray seas attack, lick ice cream   posters
off the hoardings on the pier, and facia signs
in blue and pink dedicate a railway
gouged from sea and cliff.

A love meter sulks behind locked glass.
I long to press in a coin which heats my palm.
"Please tell me what the future brings?"
Dexter lifts his leg, Tom shrugs, points
to an early wallflower on the Prom, says
"There's always hope in Spring."

BY REQUEST

No flowers
for one who knew the scent
of Dame's Violet in the hedge.

No psalms
for one who could tell
a Marsh Warbler from a Sedge.

No friends
for one who had at least a score
but, wanting to die alone,
banned them at the end.

No ritual
except the man of God, his wife
and I who knelt, ignoring her requests,
committed her to God against
piped organ sound.

We turned to go
and there she was beside me,
climbing an upland tor
pausing to claim the view.

GARDEN

Moss bound as a Devon wood,
gloomy as a graveyard
with its austere Victorian look,
wrong side of the track.

Battered by winds from the Teign,
Easterlies rape ripe shrubs,
shaded by clay brick terraces
bereft of sun, and back-to-back.

April brings a fleeting gleam
aslant a gap in granite walls
to creep at will, make its way
through my kitchen door.

Deck chairs lurk with spiders,
sleeping butterflies, rusting tools,
wait with me for June then, sun high,
emerge to work among Spring blooms
and I, in an old straw hat,
clutch coffee, book and cat,
move   determinedly
from patch to patch.

TEENAGER

You wear your mascara
like a flag of defiance;
I shout at black fringed
baby blue eyes.

You toss thick brown hair;
rock the family car
as you slam the door.

Tripping in blue split skirt
on forbidden heels down
corridors, making dents

In masculine hearts, authority,
floors. Sweeping up hours
in a hair salon

Experiencing work,
then, riding a motorbike
with a boy called John.

Those earrings - disgusting
your Dad says, but you just shrug,
shooting cheap crescents

Up towards the stars and moon.
Firmly lock the bathroom door.
Make a rainbow head.

We exchange looks, bite tongues
dreading the moment you carry
our hearts through the door
for the very last time.

HALLO OLD WOMAN

Her voice floated back,
a child with a thick
brown plait, skipping
past me on the stair
steps free as zephyred air;
no-one else was near.

My heart beat in time
to her youthful dance
remembering
a time I looked fair,
body light, hair bright,
holding dreams of chance.

But though my years span
six and three - her words -
"Hallo, old woman"
can't mean me!

COUNTRY WEEKEND BLUES

I've got those country weekend blues;
there's straw in my hair and muck on my shoes;
no bus, no gas, no proper loos

but a grand view of the moor
and a right of way past the door
which puts me in touch

        with the locals.

I've got those country weekend blues;
crickets chirp all night long,
dawn comes up like a gong,

tradition is law, and at the end of the day,
there's nothing to do
but go down to 'The Bull'

        and drink up real ale with the locals.

I've got those country weekend blues;
there's soft rain for my hair
and gallons of fresh air

if you're not downwind of the pigsty.
I ride out to hounds, dive head-first from my
horse,
break bones on hard ground,

        trying to fit in with the locals.

I've got those country weekend blues;
no bus, no gas, no proper loos,
but that right of way past the door

heading straight for the moor
through acres of mud, past recalcitrant bulls
to a fog hidden tor,

and I've fallen in love with a local.

WOMAN'S PLACE

1914 Posters grew on public walls.
   A finger pointed *Your Country Needs You*.
   She dried her tears and joined the queue,
   packing shells, making guns, waiting
   for front line messages to come.

1918 Posters grew on public walls
   advertising 'Jobs for Heroes'.
   She left her bench and joined the queue,
   seeking advice from Government departments.
   'Woman's place is in the home'.

1939 Radio channelled the message anew,
   tanks fight cavalry in Eastern Europe.
   'All men report to your nearest depot'.
   Women are needed to pack shells, make guns,
   wait for front line messages to come.

1945 Radio channelled the winning news,
   three great powers have reached Berlin.
   She left her bench and joined the queue,
   seeking advice from Government departments.
   'Woman's place is in the home'.

1966 Prosperity for the nuclear family;
   average children number almost three;
   public opinion says
   'Your children need you' to run homes.
   To put an end to latchkey children.

1986 Twenty years on the media says
     'Times have changed, industry needs you'.
     She dries her eyes and joins the queue
     for training workshops; public shares
     or benefit shoes. 'Is woman's place still in the home?'.

1990 New decade and a falling birthrate.
     'Women are needed, that means you'
     to stack shelves, wield tools, while
     New Age man cooks food, washes clothes,
     cares for children.

1995 Redundancies, and women become executives.
     Man nurses, cooks, and cleans the home.
     Shares the birth and care of children,
     takes his place with woman in the home.

THE PINGER BRINGER

Crisis came one Monday
when, deep in coffee and
chocolate biks, Trudie
was telling us about
her latest trip.

We sat, rivetted,
clutching our rejection slips
as we went over the Niagara
in a barrel, ate french fries,
sorry, I mean chips.

Annie had had a wedding,
we walked the aisle
step by step, Suzie's
grandchild was next
on the list.

Menopause, sex, M.E.';
walks on Dartmoor;
London exhibitions;
opera; literary bits
from the Sunday papers,

the latest media hits.
Is that the time?
Good gracious! Our
chairperson banged
her fist -